my mindful day

Being Present

Published in the United States of America by Cherry Lake Publishing
Ann Arbor, Michigan
www.cherrylakepublishing.com

Reading Adviser: Marla Conn, MS, Ed., Literacy specialist, Read-Ability, Inc.
Book Designer: Jennifer Wahi
Illustrator: Jeff Bane

Photo Credits: ©Aji Ardiles/Shutterstock, 5; ©stockfour/Shutterstock, 7; ©Samuel Borges Photography/Shutterstock, 9; ©fizkes/Shutterstock, 11; ©Vitalinka/Shutterstock, 13; ©terng99/Shutterstock, 15; ©wavebreakmedia/Shutterstock, 17; ©Monkey Business Images/Shutterstock, 19; ©Pixel-Shot/Shutterstock, 21; ©Rawpixel.com/Shutterstock, 23; Cover, 6, 10, 18, Jeff Bane; Various vector images throughout courtesy of Shutterstock.com

Library of Congress Cataloging-in-Publication Data has been filed and is available at catalog.loc.gov

Printed in the United States of America

table of contents

About the author: Katie Marsico is the author of more than 200 reference books for children and young adults. She lives with her husband and six children near Chicago, Illinois.

About the illustrator: Jeff Bane and his two business partners own a studio along the American River in Folsom, California, home of the 1849 Gold Rush. When Jeff's not sketching or illustrating for clients, he's either swimming or kayaking in the river to relax.

"Hello . . . are you there?"

You're out playing with a friend.

But your mind is wandering.

You should **focus** on your friend.

Yet there's a math test Monday.

And a big game next week!

Slow down!

It's fine to plan.

Still, we should be part of the **present**.

We worry too much about the **future**.

We have what we need to be **content** now.

Being present is choosing not to rush.

We make the most of the moment we're in.

It's like taking a deep breath.

People aren't always **mindful** of **emotions**.

When we're present, we pause.

We let ourselves feel more.

We think about what causes our feelings.

When was the last time you paused?

Being present also helps us listen.

We’re more mindful of others’ feelings.

This helps us get along better.

When was a time you listened to a friend?

Sometimes being present is hard.

We’re used to cell phones and computers.

We think and move fast.

People practice being present.

They **meditate** and do **yoga**.

They set aside electronics.

So much is possible in this moment!

So much is already happening!

By being present, we become part of it.

How can you be mindful today?

glossary & index

glossary

content (kuhn-TENT) happy in a peaceful, accepting way

emotions (ih-MOH-shuhnz) feelings

focus (FOH-kuhs) to give your attention to

future (FYOO-chur) the time yet to come

meditate (MED-ih-tate) to train your mind to relax and focus

mindful (MINDE-ful) aware of your body, mind, and feelings

present (PREZ-uhnt) part of this moment in time

yoga (YOH-guh) poses, breathing, and sometimes meditation and chanting that provide balance and good health

index